These poems are so intensely personal and yet their greatness lies in the universal truths they reveal. About love. About grief. About longing and anger and desire and passion…. [Each poem is] a clarion call—reminding us to count our blessings and hold fast to the now.

—Dora Rose, Deputy Director, League of Women Voters of California

"I want to take you all in/ before you're gone/ Because deep down/ I know/ I know," Matt Bialer laments in "Weeds." He knows, in spite of the heroic measures and brave fronts, that this fight they will lose. Cancer takes Matt's great love, his wife, Lenora, and this loss has produced great poetry, elegiac, gut-wrenching. If there can ever be such a thing as a silver lining wrought from devastating grief, *Always Say Goodnight* has found it. This gorgeous, must-read collection shines a brilliant light on what it means to truly love.

—Alexis Rhone Fancher, author of *The Dead Kid Poems* (2019) and poetry editor of *Cultural Weekly*

Quotidian moments of grief are preserved in these poems like insects in amber, each one made special and permanent and held in its own place, so beautifully. Read them to be reminded of the impermanence of life and the mission we all have to appreciate moments, ordinary as they may seem, that we are gifted with those we love.

—Elizabeth Cohen, professor of creative writing at SUNY Plattsburgh, and author of six poetry books, most recently *The Patron Saint of Cauliflower* (2018)

Matthew Bialer's *Always Say Goodnight* presents an astonishing and intimate bereavement in the form of the lyric address. These poems, in their detailed and affecting diction, bring us Bialer's late wife Lenora, a distinguished civil-rights lawyer and activist whose legacy is inspirational; thus we face the "ourselves" of Bialer and his daughter, Izzy, cast into a place of profound loss, mourning, and daily negotiations of coping. Now in the club nobody chooses, Bialer asks at a bereavement group, "What am I doing here?" His collection of elegies plots a course with an avowing intensity one can only build in poems of this length and scale. With their deft lineation, their enfolding "deep rumble" of insights and observations, and reluctances that are painful to confront, such as the awful DNR form, these fierce poems offer a testimony we readily turn to.

> —Prageeta Sharma, English professor at Pomona College and author
> of five poetry collections, most recently *Grief Sequence* (2019)

I've read/ that grief must/ be faced head on/ no shortcuts…" And that is exactly what Bialer accomplishes in this deeply personal and candid work. *Always Say Good Night* is not only a stunning tribute to his beloved late wife but also an excavation of excruciating loss and familial bonds. The reader is quickly drawn into keenly observed memories that fire with an intimate and collective resonance. We stand inside the heart of these poems accompanying Bialer each step of the way. By the time he writes, *"I want to take you all in/ because deep down/ I know/ I know/ You're a rose/ I can't stop looking at,"* the reader too can't bear to look away. The fragility of life seems ever more palpable and the beauty of love ever more enduring. This honest and reflective collection will indeed become a go-to resource in my psychotherapy practice for clients suffering from grief.

> —Loretta Oleck, Clinical Psychotherapist and author of *Songs From
> the Black Hole* (2016)

After a string of strangely beautiful books about the supernatural, Bialer brings his eye for salient detail and for emotional connections to his own life. Here is his trademark voice, which is searching, headlong, incantatory. Here is his artist's eye for the power that lies in the mundane. Here is a terribly sad book that I know he wishes he hadn't had to write. No one wants to have to write poems like these. But it is also a powerful book, and will make you think about your own life differently.

—Matthew Rohrer, author of eight books, most recently *The Sky Contains the Plans* (April 2020); and recipient of the Hopwood Award for poetry and a Pushcart prize

ALWAYS

SAY GOODNIGHT

Elegies for Lenora

MATT BIALER

Always Say Goodnight: Elegies for Lenora
By Matt Bialer

ISBN: 978-0-9980375-9-2

Library of Congress Control Number: 2019920781

Publication date: March 2020

Published by KYSO Flash Press: http://www.kysoflash.com
Bellingham, Washington, USA. Printed in the USA.

For our daughter, Isabel (Izzy) Bialer Lapidus

Thank you for being the inspiring, gifted human that you are.
You never cease to make me proud. You are so brave.

I know these poems are hard for you, but I hope you can engage
in them some day. They are also a celebration of a life and
you might learn some new things about Mama.

Also by Matt Bialer

1. *A Moment's Notice* [a photographic monograph with foreword by D. Foy] (Les Editions du Zaporogue, 2016)
2. *Ark: An Epic Poem in XII Parts* (Black Coffee Press, 2012)
3. *Ascent: A Book of Poetry* (Bizarro Pulp Press, 2014)
4. *Black Powder* [an epic poem] (Black Coffe Press, 2013)
5. *Breathing Darkness: An Epic Poem* (Bizarro Pulp Press, 2019)
6. *Bridge: Long Poems of the Extraordinary* (Leaky Boot Press, 2013)
7. *Distant Shores: A Poem* (Villipede Publications, 2016)
8. *Formation: An Epic Poem* (Weirdo Magnet, 2016)
9. *Frequencies: An Epic Poem* (Leaky Boot Press, 2015)
10. *Ghost Hole: An Epic Poem* (Leaky Boot Press, 2020)
11. *He Walks on All Fours: Poems* (Dynatox Ministries, 2015)
12. *Kings of Men: An Epic Poem* (Dynatox Ministries, 2015)
13. *More Than You Know* [a photographic monograph] (Les Editions du Zaporogue, 2011)
14. *Radius* (Les Editions du Zaporogue, 2011)
15. *Shadowbrook* [a book of paintings] (Les Editions du Zaporogue, 2012)
16. *Tell Them What I Saw* (PS Publishing, 2014)
17. *The Valley of the Eight: An Epic Poem* (Leaky Boot Press, 2017)
18. *Third Eye of the Inner Light: An Epic Poem* (Leaky Boot Press, 2018)
19. *Wing of Light: Poems* (Les Editions du Zaporogue, 2015)
20. *Wonder Weavers: An Epic Poem* (Bizarro Pulp Press, 2016)

Table of Contents

Come Medicine Buddha
Come shine your rays upon me
Penetrate deep within my body
To quell my queasy stomach
And soothe my aching bones

—from "Does the Buddha Play Pool?"
    a poem in the book *Diagnosis* by Lenora Lapidus

Foreword

There are no right words to deal with death and the loss of a companion. There are no right words to describe the limit of language, when it fails to encompass what is beyond its range. There are no right words either to perpetuate a portrait of the living, as they slowly fade away like old photographs. No, there are no right words, and yet. And yet. Poetry, because it it is intimately linked with music, has the magic power of expressing the unutterable, of evoking the dead as a living being, of replacing absence with a comforting ghost. Of course, it takes an incredible talent to craft words that will defeat the limits of expression and not become empty *cliché* one sends as condolences for a distant relative's funeral. Donne, Tennyson, Dickinson, Williams were such poets, whose verses dug deep in the soul, hurting and soothing at the same time, in this paradoxical chaos that Death (and sometimes Love) creates. In *Always Say Goodnight*, Matt Bialer manages to convey a tribute to his beloved late wife, Lenora, while also conjuring a form of hope through the description of the banal and trivial of every day's life. What remains is what makes us remember and move forward. These poems are also for Matt and Lenora's daughter, Izzy, a legacy she can proudly take with her and cherish. As for us, the readers, we are offered a beautiful and moving ode to love and loss, inextricably tied together in what we we call, in loss of other words, life.

—Seb Doubinsky
November 2019

Bilingual French poet, novelist, and academic Seb Doubinsky was born in Paris in 1963. His writing is published both in France and the USA. His novels, all set in a dystopian universe revolving around competing city-states, have been published in the UK and the USA. He currently lives with his family in Denmark, where he teaches French literature, culture, and history at the French department of the University of Aarhus.

Then I realized that the hardship
was a signpost:

I should do
  Something   important   with my life

—from "The Path Toward Healing," a poem
   in the book *Diagnosis* by Lenora Lapidus

Things I Would Tell You

Over three hundred people
at your funeral
standing room only
You got a huge
New York Times obituary
just about
a full page
Hillary Clinton
wrote me a letter
I thought
it was spam
until I saw Izzy's name

Lenora was a brilliant lawyer
a fierce advocate
and a remarkable woman
whose thirty years of leadership
at the ACLU
will long serve
as her enduring legacy. . .
As you and Izzy
mourn her passing
and celebrate her life. . .

Until I saw
Izzy's name
I finally
bought a bicycle
rode it once
around the park
I felt rusty and inept
Mourn her passing
and celebrate her life

Con Edison came by the house
changed all of our light bulbs
replaced with halogens
for free
Save money and energy
I don't have to
change another light bulb
for twenty years
You know
how I feel about that
I have walked
in the park more times
than ever before
all because
of you
Because of you
Sometimes eight miles
in one day
by myself
with friends
old friends
I have reconnected with people
from all aspects
of our thirty-plus years
All because
of you
Because of you
your big floppy hats
chunky jewelry
your wide black-rimmed glasses
that now sit
on Izzy's bookshelf
without your face
your hefty chuckle
lifting a Cosmopolitan to your lips
every Friday night
at our favorite corner spot

Without your face
We will never
go to Asia together
Why didn't we?
You went without us
Too far away
We couldn't spare the time
Why didn't we?
Izzy got a 30
on her first ACT exam
She got the internship
at the museum
on your birthday
two weeks after
two days before
language started to fail you
Fail you
You wanted to say something
Dishwasher!
Dishwasher!
What?
What are you trying to say?
Dishwasher!
Oh you mean ginger ale!
For nausea
The stairs up
to the bedroom
were *the airport*
Language started to fail you
The doctor calls me
I ask, why is she speaking gibberish
Can she get her language back
if the chemo starts to work?
"Her liver is failing
You say gibberish
I say cognitive impairment
Where is Izzy?"

She's out with her boyfriend
"Tell her to come home now"
Until I saw Izzy's name
Why didn't we?
We never
had last words
No last words
I gave them to Izzy
You could speak clearly
just once that day
and it was to her
You rose on the couch
lit up
Izzy!
How was your day?
"It was good, Mama"
I'm sorry Izzy
I'm sorry
Without your face
your many bottles
of creams and oils
on the night table
The legal books
and exotic novels
sit there unanswered
unused
unread
A novel that just ended
in the middle
Ended

Izzy wrote me
the greatest Father's Day card
"We always have each other
I always knew
the day would come
when we would be

celebrating today
just the two of us. . .
You were there
for her
every second
of the way
and that takes so much
bravery"
Mourn her passing
and celebrate her life
I don't have to
change another light bulb
Until I saw Izzy's name
Why didn't we?

More Things I Would Tell You

—for our daughter, Izzy Bialer Lapidus

I join a bereavement group
but I last for one session
Marriages over fifty years
died suddenly
brain aneurysm
long battle with cancer
I am the only one
who isn't crying
The only one
I don't know these people
What am I doing here?
We go around the conference room
name tags
introduce ourselves
I last for one session
When it's my turn
I pull out
a framed photograph of you
Colleagues in my office
blew it up
framed it
placed it on my desk
A professional photo shoot
for your work
Your high forehead
rouged cheeks
simple, warm smile
But I am taking you home
happen to have you in my bag
I can't look at you every day

It's the photo
used in your obituary
in memorials and tributes
I had never seen it before
Never seen it before
This was my wife, I say
This was my wife
I tell them
my almost-17-year-old daughter Izzy
attends summer school
in Boston
She's doing well there
One of the elderly women in the group
"Nobody calls me
I'm lonely
I need you people
I need this group
People shouldn't ask me
what I need
they should just bring me food
I don't want to tell them
Just do something
Do something"
She points across the table
at me
"Your child
is just a baby
and I have news for you
She is not okay
She is not okay"
I am the only one
who isn't crying
I don't want to sit here
and cry
with people I don't know
I want to learn
how to cope

how to live
how to keep going
I can't look
at you every day
I last for one session
I am taking you home
I have memorized
your social security number
filled it out
on countless forms
countless
Mailed copies
of your death certificate
I am getting used to the new bicycle
which is actually used
I rode it around the park this morning
Pushups, pullups
alternating V-ups
then photography in Manhattan
Keep going every day
try to find a rhythm
A rhythm
I am in a paddle boat
on a vast ocean
paddling
moving slowly
A vast ocean
I want to learn
how to cope
how to live
I have memorized
your social security number
I unwrap
a framed collage of photos
you had custom made for me
a recent anniversary
Don't you want to hang it?

I went out of my way
I never did anything with it
never hung it
I unwrap
A vast ocean
Photos from our wedding 26 years ago
Me cradling newborn Izzy
She on your lap as a toddler
You and me
our arms around each other
so many times
A vast ocean
Early in our romance
you on my lap
a flowered dress
hugging me
hugging
caressing
I am taking you home

Island

I'm in Herald Square
with my camera
Street photography
Looking to take pictures
of the people I pass
couples holding hands
tourist families
business people
rushing to an appointment
negotiating their phones
Air Pods
Tee shirts
REMAIN CALM
LOVE
IT'S GONNA BE OKAY
Sirens
shrieking
More than one ambulance
three of them
so loud
people hold their ears
Remain Calm
I wonder
who they are saving?
Who's in trouble?
Sirens shrieking
Two days
before you died
the nurse from hospice
wanted me to sign
a DNR form
Do Not Resuscitate
I didn't want to

Counterintuitive
What about
our marriage vows
in sickness
and in health
to love
and to cherish
until we are parted by death
Do Not Resuscitate
I don't think
that's what we said
We wrote
our own vows
Support each other
Stick with each other
no matter what
No matter what
And the rabbi said
"Adonai
our God
let there soon be heard
the voices
of the loving couple
the sound of their jubilance
from their canopies
and of the youths
from their song-filled feasts"
People hold their ears
Remain Calm
Nineteen weeks
after your death
but who's counting
I attend
my new bereavement group
Good to be with others
in my predicament
to hear their points of view

their struggles
tears
but also laughter
The Hassidic man
in our group
slept in a separate bed
from his wife
six kids
ages 6 to 28
two married
Collages of her
on the walls
blown-up photos
spray painted
a red heart
over her bed
Two months
after she passed
"It's how I survive
It's how I keep her"
The rabbi told him
"Stop this craziness"
two months after
"Stop this craziness
It's time to move on"
Sirens
shriek
Remain Calm
A woman in the group
husband gone seven months
says she's
always running
Always running
Not as in
running in the park
but running on trips
Rome

Amsterdam
"I guilt my girlfriends
into going with me
guilt them"
Another time
taking her young children
to Paris
Running on trips
I have no plans
to travel
I have no plans
I can't
because Izzy
is finishing high school
I have no plans
"Stop this craziness
It's time to move on"
Always running
Do Not Resuscitate
Another woman
in our group
always did
lots of physical sports
with her husband
all over the world
All over the world
Hikes
surfing
rock climbing
cliff dives
They were
in Indonesia
when he died
From the Greek
"Indos"
means India
"Nesos"

means island
Comprised
of 18,110 islands
more than 6,000
of them uninhabited
Ocean's calm
translucent surface
Active volcanos
grade into swamps
lowlands
shallow Java Sea
Decades of purges
and coups
violent secessionist movement
But you wouldn't know it here
so peaceful
a paradise
They were hiking
along the Kinabatangan River
in Sabah, Borneo
Ancient rainforest
temples
orangutans
clouded leopards
They spotted elephants
by the river
Borneo pygmy elephants
a rare sighting
They felt grateful
and blessed
But later
after surfing
Mentawai Islands
an archipelago
off the coast
of West Sumatra
waves

up to 15 feet tall
They're on the beach
Her husband
collapses
Dial 118
Takes an hour
for an ambulance
to come
Takes an hour
Not well equipped
doesn't look like
an ambulance
They don't
have the same level
of paramedical training
as elsewhere
in the developed world
It's too late
Too late
She wants
to take him home
hassles with the authorities
leaves their 70-kilo bags behind
told by someone
"Nothing goes unused here"
Nothing
Too late
Sirens
shrieking
Remain Calm
Do Not Resuscitate
"Stop this craziness
It's time to move on"
Always running
running on trips
I have no plans
to travel

I have no plans
I am an elephant
isolated
from the herd
Lost
Nineteen weeks
after your death
but who's counting
Another in the group
afraid she'll lose
more people
Afraid
because she's a single parent now
she'll die
on her young children
I nod
in agreement
I'm more aware
something could happen to me
More aware
What would happen to Izzy?
Fear
I will lose people
Do Not Resuscitate
"Nothing goes unused here"
Nothing
Too late
Sirens
shrieking
The other day
I was supposed
to meet my close friend Jane
for a walk
in the park
She texted me
had a stomach ache
had to cancel

I'm sorry to hear that
Feel better
The next day
she texted me
"Had to go the emergency room"
Gallstones
in her gallbladder
Alarmed
I visit her
I have not been
in a hospital
since you died
I have not been
in a hospital
Familiar and strange
EKG/ECG monitor
blood pressure
She has to have
laparoscopic gallbladder surgery
cholecystectomy
to remove the gallbladder
and gallstones
several incisions
Surgeon inflates
her abdomen
with air
to see clearly
See clearly
Relieved
she's going to be okay
I want to visit again
but Izzy
is home sick
bad cold
hungry
needs orange juice
Am I at home?

No
at work
Why aren't I home
with her?
I had to work
and have to visit Jane
"Come home"
I will early
cancel a meeting
Sirens
shrieking
Do Not Resuscitate
DNR form
purpose of informing
and instructing paramedics
EMS
hospital physicians
and medical staff
to forgo
any resuscitation attempts
Forgo
in the event
of cardiopulmonary
or respiratory arrest
I reluctantly sign it
In sickness
and in health
to love
and to cherish
"The voices
of the loving couple
and of the youths
from their song-filled feasts"
"Nothing goes unused here"
Nothing
Do Not Resuscitate
"Stop the craziness

It's time to move on"
Remain Calm
Nineteen weeks
after your death
but who's counting
I open the second drawer
of your night table
filled to the top
prescription bottles
You were a pacifist
but this was
your war chest
your secessionist movement
Tramadol
Escitalopram
Letrozole
Quetiapine
and more
Your war chest
I am an elephant
isolated
from the herd
Lost
I want to see clearly
see clearly
Always running
running on trips
I have no plans
to travel
I have no plans
When Izzy
visited Tanzania
last summer
she went on safari
saw elephants
learned about
deep rumble

communicating over great distances
sharing our human awareness
of family bonds
community
recognizing
the bones
of a loved one
A herd
against the backdrop
of ice-capped Kilimanjaro
A little one
runs for a river
so excited
about the cool water
trunk wobbled
like jelly
Like jelly
I am meeting parent friends
Austrian restaurant
for dinner
I arrive early
Hostess asks if we have a reservation
No we don't
"How many will you be?"
Six
When the first of two couples arrives
my friend Sarah
asks do we have a table
I say yes, for six
"But's it's for five"
She sees the realization
on my face
frustration
I'm sorry
"It's okay"
I oddly forgot
Do Not Resuscitate

I want to see clearly
I'm in a small turboprop plane
flying over islands
I'm lost
in the fog
Lost
No instrument rating
cannot navigate
don't know
if I'm up or down
Looking for land
an island
an air strip
a place to land
The *Twilight Zone* episode
jet airliner
a flash of light
severe turbulence
unable to contact
anyone on the ground
no radio
Descend below the clouds
identify the coastline
Manhattan Island
but there is no city
no buildings
just forest
and grazing dinosaurs
They go back up
increase altitude
to catch the same
freak jet stream
hopefully return home
Return home
Captain
addresses the passengers
"All I ask

is that you remain calm"
Flying over islands
I'm lost
in the fog
Lost
Looking for an island
an air strip
a place to land
where I'll see
an elephant
on the beach
Ocean's calm
translucent surface
An elephant
on the beach
stroking
the bleached bones
long dead companion
trunk lingering
over the skull
tenderly

Against the Current

When I come back
to the office
even though
I have been gone
for only a month
it feels like years
Years
Two weeks
after you're gone
Feels like years
I have just come back
from a war
that we lost
in a wheelchair
Fragile
wounded
I stare at my desk
which has been straightened out
School photos of Izzy
and my colleagues
blew up a photo of you
the one
from your obituary
You smile at me
but it haunts me now
How many times
have I looked
at that smile?
How many times?
I glare
at my office phone
Realization sinks in
that you will

never call me again
I will never see
the caller ID
with AM CIVIL LIBERTIES again
You will never call me
What an odd thought
I know you are gone
so of course
you will never call me again
But this is
a new
and sad revelation
Did I expect
a disembodied voice
to call?
It's just that
we used to talk
many times a day
if only for a moment
just to check in
or what's for dinner?
When will each of us come home?
One of the assistants says
she will miss your lively cheerful voice
on the line
Never call me again
People are happy
to see me back
but it's different now
Different
I'm wounded
fragile
handicapped
not myself
You barely ever came here
so I need
to claim this from you

this place
where I spend
a lot of time
I have no focus
I can't trust
my short term memory
I write reminders to myself
I read that's what grief does
Loss of focus
and memory
what you are about to do
but can't remember
Memory
Memories
I've read
that grief must
be faced head on
no shortcuts
No shortcuts
Head on
like you always do
Face things head on
Memory
Memories
So many grief books
are pitifully bad
Hallmark cards
shallow
obvious
simplistic
too religious
for me
Too religious
Never call me again
No caller ID
I think of calling
your office number

just to see
if your voice
is still there
on the voicemail
A disembodied voice
But I can't
And when I try
a week later
it's gone
another part of you
that has disappeared
One big vanishing act
A disembodied voice
All I can really do
is just stare
out the window
Great view of the Hudson
from the 15th floor
In the winter
I watch the sun
fall behind
the skyscrapers
glass towers
across the river
Jersey City
The sun
almost electrifies them
massive columns
of burning circuitry
Never call me again
I'm wounded
fragile
handicapped
not myself
Memory
Memories
A disembodied voice

I stare out the window
When I make
conference calls
I turn away
from my desk
and computer
and stare out the window
so I'm not distracted
Sometimes
I see hawks circling
over the city
circling
or children running around
a rooftop playground
I think of when we
used to bring Izzy
to the playground
She loved hanging upside down
on the monkey bars
I remember one day
I was on a call
staring out the window
I saw a bunch of helicopters
following something
floating down the Hudson
Following something
I wondered what it was
But I forgot about it
until I read
on my computer
about the Miracle on the Hudson
January 5, 2009
US Airways Flight 1549
Airbus A320
in climb-out after takeoff
from La Guardia Airport
strikes a flock

of Canada geese
northeast
of the George Washington Bridge
loses all engine power
Unable to reach
any airport
Captain Chesley "Sully" Sullenberger
glides his plane
to a ditching
in the Hudson River
off midtown Manhattan
I had seen the plane
drifting past
drifting past
with all of those helicopters
then disappear
I call you
Did you hear
about the airliner
that landed in the Hudson?
No, I haven't
Been a little busy today
Look at the news
I saw the plane
drift down the river
I saw it from my window
drifting
You yourself always
go against the current
Against the current
Whether it is
your women's rights work
from custodians
to nail salon workers
to women in combat roles
you understand
that advocating women's rights

needs to be broader
than just a focus
on white collar
professional women
In a restaurant
No, I don't like this table
How about that one?
Tasting cocktails
Too sweet
Too strong
Too tangy
In a movie theater
I don't like these seats
Let's switch
You like to boast
that your parents
brought you in a backpack
to Martin Luther King Jr's
I HAVE A DREAM speech
that your mother
was one of the first to breast feed
and did not shave
her armpits
Fifth grade
there was a psychological exercise
in brainwashing
and authoritarianism
Everyone had to wear an A
on their foreheads
You started making Ps
P for the People
and recruited students
for the rebellion
I have no focus
I can't trust
my short term memory
I write reminders to myself

I read that's what grief does
Loss of focus
and memory
what you are about to do
but can't remember
Memory
Memories
I've read
that grief must
be faced head on
No shortcuts
Ten days
after you're gone
I visit your office
125 Broad Street
downtown
by South Street Seaport
right on the East River
I go to Human Resources
to find out
about your benefits
401K
pension
back pay for unused sick days
vacation days
life insurance
Afterwards
I go to the 17th floor
to visit your colleagues
your peeps
say hello
There are notes
on your office door
outpourings
testimonials
sadness
respect

I go into your office
Someone says to me
"You have not been here
in years, have you?"
No, I haven't
Maybe when she got an award
Signs
BREAKING DOWN BARRIERS
FIGHTING FOR JUSTICE
Law books
Photos of Izzy
Photos of us
Photos of your hero
a young Ruth Bader Ginsburg
A large illustration
of you before the Supreme Court
Another sign
LOVE TRUMPS HATE
Black and white photo
from our wedding
you and your mother dancing
You're both gone now
A black and white
I took in Lucca, Italy
a woman sitting on church steps
Pigeons fly
and scatter in front of her
I was always
looking for a perfect
pigeons-in-flight shot
and we thought I got one
And you wanted it
to remind you
of your trips
Your ceramics
on your crammed desk
Never call me again

Someone says
"We'll go through her office"
I only want the personal stuff
not the law books
And if you find
her letters from Ruth Bader Ginsburg
I would like them
for Izzy
They ask if I would like
to stay for lunch
but I'm too sad
Too sad
They never find those letters
A few weeks later
huge boxes arrive from UPS
nine of them
Some of them say
FRAGILE
GLASS
Izzy comes home
"What are those?"
Mama's office
"Get them away from me"
I think of your now-empty office
another part of you
that has disappeared
One big vanishing act
A disembodied voice
Never call me again
I bring the boxes
to the basement
Fragile
I can hear broken pieces
rattling inside one of them
In a wheelchair
Fragile
Wounded

I'm in a jet fighter
that was shot down
over water
during a war
A war that we lost
Glass towers blazing
shattering
like the sun
has burst
Burst
Everything is on fire
even the water itself
I'm drifting helplessly
disappearing
down the river
And I'm burning

So Happy in Your Kayak

You are so happy
in your kayak
bright red
I help you get it
in the water
Because of your back
hard for you
to do it yourself
You are so happy
in your kayak
Why don't you
come with me?
That's okay
next time
The fact is
I don't like
to go out
for as long
as you do
I want to read
or paint
or write
or just behold the lake
water reflecting
the gentle hills
the wind
the currents
Everything
is pulsating
emanating
I like to stare at it
for my own peace of mind
for my watercolor landscape painting

Why don't you
come with me?
I will next time
I love to see you off
with your kayak
big floppy hat
sunglasses
your phone
It's the only time
I ever see you
so thrilled
free
relaxed
Work always
hangs over you
I like to
drink this in
Nothing else matters
It's a week day
There are few boats
And if it is
not windy
the lake is like glass
Hills
Sailboats
Sea gulls
You are so happy
in your kayak
A green and blue
looking glass
And you will
come back
with stories
and photographs
A great blue heron
turtles
ducks

some folks
who tossed you
a beer from their dock
You could be gone
for hours
your floppy hat
sunglasses
infectious smile
hefty chuckle
Text me
when you come back
so I can help you
lug the kayak out
Sometimes
I do go with you
in my blue kayak
August
Our two weeks
up here
Country house
in the Berkshires
Izzy away at camp
We glide
to the other side
of the lake
around the island
It's like
we're under a spell
A spell
All time ceases
The current
hypnotizes
Don't damage
the water lilies
And we cruise
into the inlet
Many houses

and docks
and sometimes
a turtle
sunbathing on a log
We admire
a big magnificent white birch
leaning
queen of the bank
unofficially our tree
Always
drawn to it
Drawn to it
We're under a spell
a spell
All time ceases
hypnotizes
We chat
with folks
on their docks
gossip about the lake
You do
most of the talking
for us
Are they finally
going to dredge the lake?
Silt
and invasive weeds
Eurasian milfoil
No they can't
until they figure out
a way to protect the snails
We all giggle
Another thing
that gives you
a thrill
downhill skiing
Until the doctor

tells you
this has to stop
to stop
You grew up skiing
with your late dad
Very tender memories
for you
Tender memories
I took up skiing again
because of you
You hate the cold
but it could be
ten below
you don't care
Transformed
charged
and impervious
to the cold
A snow globe
of mountains
the Alps
Besides your
civil rights work
you are the most fearless
on the slopes
Your light blue
one-piece snow suit
Black diamond runs
moguls
carving
You're a ripper
down the slopes
perfect parallel turns
Nothing
is off limits
Nothing
You were

on the ski team
at Cornell
We would ski
in Vermont
with friends from my work
Phil was a good skier too
But he would smile
admire your deftness
Your wife
she can ski
you not so much
and we would both laugh
A snow globe
of mountains
the Alps
You teach Izzy
to ski
Until the doctor
tells you
this has to stop
to stop
You feel guilty
that you're not
taking her skiing
To you
it's malnourishment
It's okay I say
she doesn't love it
as much as you
It's okay
Another thing
you love to do
press flowers
For a few years
until Izzy was born
you bought these wooden presses
blank cards

experimented with different shellacs
made cards for friends
family
in the Berkshires
You loved Queen Anne's lace the most
white
so intricate
and delicate
Tuolumne Meadows
Yosemite National Park
You were ecstatic
The flowers
were raining down
everywhere
petal parachutes
And you needed
to snatch them
for your press
to capture
shooting stars
purple lupines
yellow monkey-flowers
paintbrushes
poppies
yellow fiddlenecks
redbuds
You picked them
for your press
Um I think I read
that some of these flowers
are protected
But you didn't care
It was the rebel in you
the one
that used to shoplift
in junior high school
Bend the rules

see what you can
get away with
Mischief maker
We were driving outside
Yosemite
You shouted
Stop the car!
You ran out
stood over
a big yellow flower
glanced around
to make sure
no one was looking
picked it
stuffed it into your press
But the flower was too big
You were giggling
Flowers rained down everywhere
petal parachutes
and you needed to
snatch them
for your press
You stopped
when Izzy was born
You talk
of picking it up again
but you never do
You never do
Izzy and I
are on the lake
She's in your red kayak
gliding around
looking for signs
of you
a message
Maybe we'll see
an owl

or a great blue heron
"Mama loved herons"
You are so happy
in your kayak
We paddle
into the inlet
Izzy looks at me
"What's wrong, Daddy?"
I'm staring
at the birch
which has broken
fallen
into the water
Fallen
Two months
after you're gone
my sister and I
are going through the basement
of the country house
Rubbish removal
1-800-GOT-JUNK
We throw away
Izzy's old puppet theatre
which she hardly used
her art easel
an old ping pong table
cracked computer monitor
I come across our skis
As much as it pains me
I toss them
yours and mine
As much as it pains me
we find your
flower presses
behind other stuff
on a shelf
No, we keep those

I have to keep them
I look at them
I can see that big yellow flower
from Yosemite
My eyes moisten
and I escape upstairs
Later
my sister tells me
she found more presses
and put them all
in one good place
on the shelf
Why don't you
come with me?
For all too briefly
I captured a flower

Yellow

Before we
go to the doctor
I help dress you
and bring you
down the stairs
You hold your belly
joke *I feel like I'm pregnant*
but you're not
Distended liver
Feels like your stomach
is being stretched
And your feet are swollen
stumps
I am trying to get socks
on them
None of your shoes fit
and you have so many pairs
I'll find shoes
for swollen feet later
Get a shoe horn
I have a composition notebook
like the kind from elementary school
Charts for all of the pills
what the pills are
what they're for
how many times a day
date
time of day
I write notes to myself too
More ginger candy for nausea
Prune juice
Ginger ale
More heating pads

Shoes
Shoe horn
Distended liver
and your feet are swollen
When we get
to the cancer center
I put you in a wheelchair
Not the first time I have
Seven years ago
when your spine partially collapsed
You don't have the strength
to walk across a hall
I wait in reception
while a nurse
takes you
to the examination room
I'm on my phone
nervous
afraid of bad news
On Amazon
here are the shoes
Secret Slippers
Women's Air Cushion
breathable
adjustable
walking shoes
comfy
elderly
I place the order
to be delivered Thursday
Today is Tuesday
Feels like forever
In this universe
you're still
in the examination room
This is taking too long
Too long

Distended liver
and your feet are swollen
I'm nervous
afraid of bad news
I think my hand is shaking
You've always rallied
Always rallied
Even when the odds are against
Why not this time?
But this feels different
Different
And I can't show you
my fear
Can't show you
Have to be strong
You text me
Go to his office
I walk in
and you're both there
Where's Debbie?
The nurse practitioner
we like her
warm and real
"You're stuck with just me today"
He reminds me of Bernie Sanders
old curmudgeon
But you two
have a nice rapport
and he loves your civil rights fights
knows all about Izzy
He sits behind his desk
shaking his head
typing furiously on his computer
"You say you are feeling better
and I don't know why"
Distended liver
and your feet are swollen

"I recommend that we stop treatment
but knowing you
you'll want to continue
Am I right?"
We both say yes in unison
"Gee, what a surprise!
What a surprise!"
But the doctor
gives me a look
when you turn away
Gives me a look
I'm frightened
It's the look
that says
Buckle up
Buckle up
There will be nothing
left standing
Nothing left standing
At the chemo infusion center
you see Mary
your favorite nurse
sweet, motherly
Irish
How will I know?
"You'll just know dearie"
The next day
you're lying on the couch downstairs
Alexandria
our cleaning person arrives
She looks at you
looks at me
concerned
and sad
Concerned
and sad
You're holding your belly

with a heating pad
I ordered shoes for you
You're looking
at a big watercolor by me
on the wall
a marsh
lots of bright colors
cadmium yellow
opera red
violet
French ultramarine
I love that painting
It always soothes me
I'm glad it does
This isn't fair to you
Don't say that
It's what I signed up for
But it's true
It's not fair
Please don't say that
You're not going to work
It doesn't matter
Well, we are *spending*
A lot of time together
I like that
How will I know?
Distended liver
and your feet are swollen
I'm tired of this
Please don't say that
You've never said that before
But I am
I beg of you not to say that
for Izzy's sake
Izzy is supposed
to get an Honors Society Science Award
at school

You want to go with me
but we both know you can't
You can't
I ask Alexandria
if she would stay
while I go uptown
to see Izzy receive the award
How will I know?
When I get back
Debbie the nurse practitioner
calls me
If they're calling me
I know it's bad
They always talk to you
I go to the basement
so you won't hear
You're sleeping anyway
"Sorry I wasn't there yesterday
But I looked at her chart

You have to start hospice"
What?
"You have to start hospice"
I don't know
I can't
I have to talk to her
I have to talk to Izzy
Let's say the chemo
starts working?
"Then we stop it
But her chart
It doesn't look good"
I don't know
I'll think about it
"You have to start hospice"
Distended liver
and your feet are swollen
How will I know?
There will be nothing
left standing
Nothing left standing
I can hardly get you
up the stairs anymore
to go to sleep
I use all of my weight
All of my weight
to push you up
When you sleep
you groan loudly
guttural sound
animal
something other
taking over
Something other
some maleficent creature
possessing you
I go downstairs

to sleep on the couch
But I can't sleep
The sound alarms me
Can't sleep
"You have to start hospice"
The next day
I get you
down the stairs
You're trying to work
holding your phone
Your skin is yellow
Jaundice
a word I have encountered
from afar
but here it is
saying hello
Jaundice
And you see
a look of dismay
on my face
that I failed
to hide
What?
Nothing
What is it?
You know me
too well
Can't sleep
Whites of your eyes
are yellow
Bilirubin
yellow colored
waste material
toxins
related to the liver
I try to think
of animals

with yellow eyes
Cats
Raccoons
Owls
Anything to reassure myself
Distended liver
and your feet are swollen
"You have to start hospice"
Buckle up
Buckle up
There will be nothing
left standing
Nothing left standing
The doorbell rings
Your shoes have arrived
How will I know?

Footsie

Summer of 2011
you get it
into your head
that you are tired
of hormonal treatments
for your breast cancer
Tired of hormones
They make you feel weird
not yourself
burning rashes
You want to try
something different
Something different
From a family friend
a prominent
breast cancer researcher
in Houston
you hear
about a clinical trial
University of Chicago
Your oncologist
who knows our friend
is ambivalent about it
I can see it on his face
He doesn't want
to argue with you
respects you too much
And that means I am too
Ambivalent
If it isn't broke
don't fix it
You can't just go by
your whim

your instincts
You are not a doctor
but you insist
I'm tired of these damned
hormonal treatments
I don't know
I don't know
You want to mix things up
It's the rebel in you
If it isn't broke
don't fix it
Izzy is in camp
We fly to Chicago
You are so winded
at the airport
Winded
Have to stop to rest
Can't catch my breath
We plan
to get you the treatment
and depart
in one day
At the University hospital
they say
you need a blood transfusion
A blood transfusion? No
But they're insistent
Red blood cell count low
It's why you are
so winded
I don't want to
It scares me
"It's perfectly safe
all blood heavily screened
Very rare
if there's a problem"
Very rare

"But it will take five hours"
Five hours
"And you will feel much better"
And so the clinical trial
will begin tomorrow
At this point
you've been ill
for seven years
and we've basically
lived our lives normally
We go to Europe on vacation
The Berkshires
All of that
is about to change
About to change
We're briefed
about the clinical trial
If it isn't broke
don't fix it
Experimental
Starve the cancer cells
Starve them
Comes in the form
of these four big ugly brown pills
Horse pills!
How can anyone swallow those?
And they taste terrible
You have been through so many treatments
taken so many drugs
I can't keep it all straight
I have a bad feeling
but I want to be supportive
You've made up your mind
You really want this
and it's your way
of taking control
being proactive

You're tired of being poked
with needles
and going to hospitals
all of the time
Screw this
Starve the cancer cells
Starve them
We fly to Chicago
once a month
They're supposed
to be monitoring you
but no one is doing scans
MRIs
And you are not
going to NYU
to see your oncologist
We even call him
by his first name Matt
Like mine
From Iowa
He always holds your hand
"I know this isn't fun"
We chose him because he is kind
and he has no social life
just work
and his dog
I have a bad feeling
you're falling below radar
Falling
I think about calling Matt
the truth of what he thinks
but I don't
Over the next few months
you start to feel bad
Your back really hurts
excruciating pain
Pain

If it isn't broke
don't fix it
Falling below radar
Falling
The truth of what he thinks
Friday night
January 2012
You're having trouble walking
You're weak
After an examination
you're waiting
at the elevator
to go home
You drop your glasses
bend down
to pick them up
And you fall
You fall
Falling below radar
You call me
at home
They are putting you
in a car
You fell
You can't walk
This is a hospital
but there are no crutches
No crutches
I meet the car
and I carry you
into the house
Your back
in acute pain
Acute
I feel like I was stabbed
You're nauseous
throwing up

Four big ugly pills
Falling below radar
Falling
The next day
I drive you
to NYU
There are no Ubers yet
For the next few weeks
we go there
three to four times a week
Three to four times a week
All day
your back
in acute pain
Nausea
can't stop throwing up
Nose bleeds
Your blood levels
dangerously low
Breast cancer cells
in your bone marrow
Calcium pouring
into your blood
making you sick
Low potassium
You can barely walk
I put you in a wheelchair
They keep trying to stabilize
Stabilize
But everything's
still not right
A few weeks later
you call down to me
from upstairs
You're on the floor
of our bathroom
You have a walker

but you fell
Blood coming out
of your nose
and ears
Okay this is enough
I feel overwhelmed
Overwhelmed
Can't even remember
last time
I went to work
I can't handle this anymore
Can't
I call the doctor
He carefully instructs me
not to call an ambulance
"They'll take her to a hospital
in Brooklyn
Call a car service instead
Go to NYU's Emergency Room
She's in their system
They'll know what to do"
You feel wretchedly sick
I've never seen
such intense nausea
A sky scream
Rollercoaster ride
You throw up again
before the car comes
I take plastic bags with me
in case you need to again
You look terrified
I make calls about Izzy
Someone has to pick her up
from school
take her for the night
Because I know you are
not coming home

for at least a few days
At least a few days
What will I tell Izzy?
We've never told her
about your illness
Never
Carefully hidden it
to protect her
Not to scare
But that will
have to change
Falling below radar
Falling
I'm informed
by a doctor
that due to breast cancer cells
throughout your bones
your spine
has partially collapsed
Partially collapsed
I feel like a wall has been torn open
thousands of termites and larvae
an infestation
Tumors everywhere
Everywhere
You've been taking morphine
but you need something stronger
That night
one of your best friends arrives
She's a social worker
for hospice
but not here as that
We meet with a palliative care person
When you hear that term
your eyes widen
alarmed
You think it's hospice

No, no, not hospice!
Eugene
the palliative care person
looks at you
stroking his chin
Afro
big toothy grin
"I'm going to take you off morphine
and put you on methadone"
Later
he smiles
looks at me quizzically
like I'm not getting something
that I don't get the bigger picture
Strokes his chin
regards me
My concern
My fatigue
My anxiety
My hope
"You know that this is
a very serious disease
don't you?"
Yes, of course
"It will eventually overwhelm her
The outcome is never good
It is a very serious disease"
I'm incensed
and also exhausted
Why is he telling me this?
I snap at him
Are you a fucking doctor?
Don't you dare
tell me this!
You're not a doctor!
Our friend intervenes
steps between us

She knows Eugene
"Please don't tell him these things"
He goes to visit you
When he comes back
he apologizes
Toothy grin
Eyes light up
My hope
Tells me that he told you
"Your husband loves you very, very much
Loves you very, very much"
Tells me that when he comes home
from the hospital
lies in bed
wife reads to him
children's books
Charlotte's Web
Little Princess
Secret Garden
The outcome is never good
Your doctor arrives at 10 p.m.
I think to myself
what a way to spend
a Friday night
in the emergency room
I ask flat out
if you're going to die
Is she going to die?
He says I don't think so
"We're going to do
a very powerful chemo
Scorched earth
But it will get worse
before it gets better"
You will lose
all of your hair
and be in a lot of pain

I leave you in the hospital
go home
pass out
Next day
I fetch Izzy
tell her that you're very ill
in the hospital
probably for days
"Is Mama going to die?"
It's not what they're telling me
Not what they're telling me
It will eventually overwhelm her
"I don't want to sleep over friends' houses
I want to be with you"
Do you want to come
to the hospital with me?
"No"
A logistical challenge
How do I visit you
and keep Izzy?
How?
When I pick you up
from the hospital
your brother helps me
He is a psychiatrist
organizes all of your medications
in a pill box
writes down when
and what they're for
The next day
you drop the box
Pills all over the floor
All over
I pick each one up
bring them to the pharmacist
and he meticulously
reorganizes them

Always says
"Anything for your wife
Anything!"
A close friend calls me
hounds me
"You need to hire a nurse
You're crazy not to
You can't do this yourself!"
When I bring you to NYU
I ask some nurses
about hiring a nurse
I know I'm exhausted
They mention the insurance company
an application process
They come and take the patient's temperature
I'm zonked
I feel like they are describing to me
how a jet engine works
I just don't have it in me
I don't
Thousands of termites and larvae
an infestation
Tumors everywhere
Everywhere
"It will eventually overwhelm her
The outcome is never good"
My friend
God bless her
interviews and hires a nurse-in-training
sends her to me
Comes in three times a week
so I get some relief
Badly needed relief
Neither of us
has been to work
in months
Months

Friends call
Many of them
don't even know
They tell me
that I have fallen off
the face of the earth
Falling below radar
Falling
And eventually
you recover
Back to work
by Memorial Day
Wear a wig
for a year
Due to damage to your spine
you've lost five inches in height
You're upset about that
We see a back surgeon
but there is nothing he can do
Nothing he can do
Your bones are too weak
I'm just happy you're alive
Happy you're alive
And now it's seven years later
Three months
after you're gone
and I don't need
to worry about
hiring nurses anymore
I hired an estate attorney
Some things are in probate
I need federal ID
for Izzy
so I renew our passports
I use blue ink
instead of black
Have to start over again

And I stapled my photo
to the wrong form
They won't accept a photo
that already had staples in it
I have to get my picture taken again
Izzy says I look so pissed off
in the photo
After four visits
I got Izzy Social Security benefits
Health insurance is a mess
I have to do a hearing
over the phone
and explain my case
I met one of your best friends
for lunch in the Berkshires
We each drove thirty miles
to the Creamery
I heard some noise
when I got out of the car
Some noise
Didn't know what it was
I shrugged
When I came back
two hours later
after our lunch
I had left our car motor running
Last night
dinner with an old friend
We talked about you
I could laugh again
Laugh again
And when I went home
I walked past
the place where we had
our first date
summer of 1988
Caffe Dante

A young couple smooching
in the window
I remember us sitting there
and your leg nuzzled mine
under the table
and I thought
You're gutsy
I like that
Then your foot
on mine
under the table
You liked to say
Didn't you know
I was playing footsie with you?
I was playing footsie

Weeds

I let the garden
go to weed
I didn't look at it
all summer
Overtaken
Overgrown
Weeds growing
out of the patio
out of control
in the side patches
I'm disappointed in myself
A corner of our world
I have failed
Failed
Should I weed it now
or just throw in the trowel
for the year?
I let the garden
go to weed
It's fall
and the dead leaves
I bagged in the spring
are still sitting there
in big black garbage bags
Sitting there
I never brought them out
I remember the day
in April
I was raking
You were ill
your liver
your last few weeks
Last few weeks

Lying on the couch
so happy I was raking
Meant it was spring
your favorite season
Your birthday not too far away
Dinner out
You already made the reservation
a great new French restaurant
you heard about
Tickets for *To Kill a Mockingbird*
the three of us
You wanted me to go out
do something
Go out with my camera
not just sit with you
all day
You need to go out
This isn't fair to you
I am where I want to be
I tell you
but I think to myself
I feel clingy
I want to take you all in
before you're gone
Because deep down
I know
I know
you're a rose
I can't stop looking at
The dead leaves
are still sitting there
I let the garden
go to weed
a corner of our world
I have failed
Failed
But I take care

of the flowers
on the deck
Petunias
and the wild seed mixture
Columbine
Shasta daisy
Purple coneflower
I take care
of the flowers
on the deck
where we both
used to sit
in our matching Adirondack chairs
we had custom built
So many bright Saturday mornings
I came down
and you put
the blue cushions
on your chair
for your bad back
from the illness
Sunglasses
Reading the paper
Emails on your phone
Just like a flower
you soaked up the sun
Soaked it up
You're a rose
I can't stop looking at
I feel clingy
I want to take you all in
The dead leaves
are still sitting there
I let the garden
go to weed
a corner of our world
I have failed

Failed
I still have your cushions
from the car
I can't throw them out
Like I can't throw out
the dead leaves
I don't know
what to do with them
I put them
in the trunk
and every time
I open it
to put bags in
I see them
Foam half-circle
for your neck
the other for your back
I feel sad
But it's a sadness
I want
A sadness
Raindrops on a weed
I don't know
what to do
with them
I let the garden
go to weed
I've taken care of
a lot of your estate stuff
Months of deep focus
which is hard
Social Security for Izzy
Your 401ks
Refinancing the mortgage
Changing the college fund
to my name
A financial advisor

New health care
The condo in New Mexico
All starting to come together
Come together
Except I let the garden
go to weed
I didn't look at it
all summer
Overtaken
Overgrown
Weeds growing
out of the patio
out of control
in the side patches
I'm disappointed in myself
A corner of our world
I have failed
Failed
There's a block party today
kids in the bouncy castle
a band cranking standards
"Rebel Rebel"
"Tempted"
"Brown-Eyed Girl"
One thing people
don't know about you
When you hear a song
on the car radio
especially from the Seventies
you know all of the lyrics
You sing along or hum
always
in the car
with your cushions behind you
Sing along
Nothing makes you happier
You don't know who wrote

or played the song
You don't care
You know all of the lyrics
You're a rose
I can't stop looking at
There's a block party today
And ordinarily
I would be outside with you
And you would chat up everybody
bouncing from neighbor to neighbor
like the kids
in the bouncy castle
Your hefty chuckle
Introducing yourself and me
talking about Izzy
I am not as social as you
and I'm hiding in the house
I don't want to talk
to people
I don't know
I don't want to pretend
that you didn't die
I don't want to pretend
but now I keep busy
go to the gym
run in the park
I'm more social
only with people I already know
I joined a new bereavement group
people our age
And I like it
ways to cope
Which is worse
sudden death
or prolonged illness?
Listening to loud angry music
while running

Signs from our loved ones
hearing their favorite songs
at Whole Foods
or on the street
Signs from our loved ones
You had so many favorites
Your birthday was approaching
less than two weeks
after you died
and days after Mother's Day
At first I can't bring myself
to honor your wishes
Go the restaurant
and see the play the next day
I can't bring myself
But then I think
I have to
I have to
I ask Izzy
Who should take your place
She says her boyfriend
which is a no-brainer
Why did I even ask?
So the three of us
honor your birthday weekend
And it feels right
And good
I feel clingy
I want to take you all in
because deep down
I know
I know
You're a rose
I can't stop looking at
Tonight I am seeing
the parents of Izzy's camp friend
up in Harlem

They're both shrinks
While we're having dinner
I wonder what they would think
I let the garden
go to weed
It's fall
and the dead leaves
I bagged in the spring
are still sitting there
in big black garbage bags
Sitting there
I never brought them out
I wonder what they would think
A rose
I can't stop looking at

About a Week

It's Friday
I bring you downstairs
for the last time
I can't get you
back upstairs anymore
You're too weak
Have you sitting
at the dining room table
You're having trouble
putting words together
knowing the names
of things
Alarming to both of us
I can't understand you much
but I look into those yellow eyes
and I can see
you have something to say
I can see your frustration
with yourself
I am trying to understand
by your quizzical eyes
By your eyes
By your eyes
Trying to get you
to eat Noosa
your favorite yogurt
You eat so little
I'm concerned
I have the composition book
with the charts
for the pills
which ones
what they're for

and when
You're not interested
in your phone anymore
The tie has been severed
A booster
separated from a rocket
falling to earth
Falling
You were constantly checking it
for work
Constantly
Sometimes to my annoyance
Not now
not anymore
You know you can't
write anymore
can't compose a sentence
You're not interested anymore
I am exhausted
have not slept much
force myself to eat
a chore
A chore
trying to feed you yogurt
by the spoonful
Please eat
Please
Started calling friends
family
Texting
My brother
is flying in from Michigan
A close friend from Berkeley, California
she says
"I am not posing this as a question
I am coming
I won't stay with you"

Others are coming
I'm exhausted
Others are coming
the cavalry
I called hospice
Someone arrives
in a blue uniform
I am not familiar with
My brother arrives
and some friends
She wants to check on you
lying on the couch
lots of pillows
a blanket
Guttural groan
sounds like a large
sleeping animal
Wants to wake you
Why?
Please don't wake her
You see all you need to know
She hands me a slick brochure
"Welcome to Hospice"
Like I just bought
a new car
Trying to follow
what she's saying
I'm too fried
and exhausted
A packet of drugs
will arrive
I am to put it
in the refrigerator
Some of them
are injections
I am to put it
in the refrigerator

Injections
Good, will a nurse come
to administer them?
"No, you have to"
Me?
"Yes, we're not allowed to
Here's a number to call
with any questions"
One of our friends
who was a social worker
for hospice
asks when is a bed coming
"She needs a bed"
"You need to call the number"
"Our friend
needs a home health aide
Look at her
Someone needs to come today"
"You need to call the number"
I sign a few forms
Your birthday
Social security number
I don't even know
what I am signing
or care
I'm too exhausted
Glad others
are pitching in
I need to think
It's beginning to unravel
Unravel
Another longtime friend
knows a home health aide
who helped her
with her mother
Ahh yes
I remember

She spoke at the funeral
a Jamaican woman
Lynda
Please ask
if she will come
She can't be alone at night
She can't be alone
Beyond me now
It's beginning to unravel
Unravel
By your eyes
By your eyes
You're not interested
in your phone anymore
The tie has been severed
A booster
separated from a rocket
falling to earth
Falling
The house is full of people
You recognize them
I can tell
by your eyes
By your eyes
Someone tries to readjust you
on the pillows
You look afraid
You point at me
want me to move you
You look afraid
Do you know?
Do you know?
Doctor calls me
now my phone buddy
"How is she?"
Not very good
talking gibberish

If this chemo works
will she get her speech back?
"It's gibberish to you
but cognitive impairment to me"
Whatever
"Her liver is failing
I can't believe
she is still alive"
I ask why
after 14 years
it's now so aggressive
"Because it has morphed
It's been aggressive for a year
Her blood levels are so low
that I can't use a stronger chemo
My hands are tied
Where is Izzy?"
She's out with her boyfriend
"Tell her to come home
She needs to be
with her mother"
She needs to be
with her mother
My hands are tied
"I can't believe
she is still alive"
It's beginning to unravel
Unravel
I am running an errand
at the pharmacy
when I see Izzy
on the sidewalk
She runs to me
hugs me
starts sobbing
"Mama's dying isn't she?
I can't believe this

I can't"
I won't answer
I can't
I can't say
too unthinkable
unspeakable
I just hug her
hug her hard
My hands are tied
The next day
you sleep most of the day
The loud moaning
Friend from California
puts lavender scent
under your nose
your favorite
I think you smile
Another on the phone
with hospice
"Where's my bed?
I need a bed!"
Another is reading
Michelle Obama's
Becoming
to you
even though you
already read it
You smile
You like it
People from your work come
Your peeps
hold your hand
read cards and letters
Get well
Get well
We look forward to having you back

Izzy walks in
asks if she can
play the piano
You perk up
become articulate
for the second
to last time
Of course you can, Izzy
I would love that
And so she plays
You smile at her
by your eyes
By your eyes
Cantor Lisa
from the temple arrives
We love her
She bat-mitzvahed Izzy
lives around the corner
a friend
beautiful singing voice
When you were very ill
seven years ago
she sang a song
"Angel"
on your voice mail
You always told her
that you kept it
Kept it
B'shem Hashem
Elohel yisrael
Sings to you
Sings
You smile
Cantor Lisa
gets up to walk away
You say your last words

More! More!
Where is that bed?
Where is that bed?
I can't believe
less than a month ago
we were at a Broadway show
and dinner with friends
Two weeks ago
at my mother's 90th birthday
at a restaurant in New Jersey
Two weeks ago
Last month
you told me
All I want to do
is just be in my kayak
this summer
Be in my kayak
this summer
"I can't believe
she's still alive"
It's all beginning to unravel
Unravel
I'm exhausted
Nothing feels real
Standing on the front stoop
with Cantor Lisa
I look at her
This is a weird question
but I don't know
anything about funerals
What to do?
Where?
I feel odd
bringing this up
while you still breathe
Still breathe

"Don't worry
I'm going to help you
I have the feeling
we're going to need
a large venue"
Later
on the phone
with hospice
Where is the bed?
Where is it?
"Coming later
And that packet of drugs
coming soon too
Remember to
put it in the refrigerator
Some of them
are injections"
I tell her
it's hard to
get her to eat
I'm really concerned
"Don't worry about that
Food doesn't matter anymore"
All I want to do
is just be in my kayak
A booster
separated from a rocket
falling to earth
Falling
Lynda comes
Relieved that she is
staying by your side tonight
Relieved
And the bed finally arrives
8 p.m.
We watch them assemble it

right by the couch
Lynda and I
lift you onto the bed
even though
you don't want to
leave the couch
In our piano room
I ask Lynda
How long does she have?
How long does she have?
"I would say
about a week"
A week
Good
I have a week
to process this
A week
I am strangely relieved
Food doesn't matter anymore
I stay up with my brother
We watch TV
Rachel Maddow
a show you and I
would watch
almost every day
sip wine
Neither of us
is paying attention
both of us
exhausted
depleted
My brother falls asleep
4:30 a.m.
Asleep in our bedroom
My brother wakes me
What?

"Lynda says it's time"
It's time?
Really?
It's time?
I wake Izzy up
We all go downstairs
My brother says
he heard commotion
an hour ago
thrashing about
I feel sad
and guilty
I should have stayed up
I've never
seen someone die
Never seen someone die
much less
the love of my life
Still some breath left
Izzy holds your hand
I put mine
on your shoulder
"We love you Mama
We love you"
We watch you
Even though
you are still breathing
you seem gone to me
Gone
A husk
Yellow jaundice
You take your last breath
quietly
Last breath
You just stop
Stop

I look at my phone
4:42 a.m.
You expire
Expire
We sit on the couch
silent
I'm numb
I don't know
what just happened
Don't know
Half an hour later
I'm still on the couch
Izzy went upstairs
Don't know where
my brother is
I'm just sitting there
Lynda called hospice
A nurse is coming
to declare you dead
Arrives
in a blue uniform
I don't recognize
Arrives
to check your pulse
I am numb
can't even think
But imagine
what a strange job
this nurse has
driving around New York City
checking on expired people
in the middle of the night
Driving around
double parking
hazard lights flashing
Shadow of death

asks time of death
Lynda says 4:30
I know it's 4:42
but I say nothing
Does it matter?
Shadow of death
The funeral home people
arrive a few hours later
Izzy
Do you want to say good-bye?
She's in bed
"No, I already did"
Watch them
put you in a body bag
zip
lift you onto a stretcher
take you away
I'm numb
exhausted
Everything strange
I've never
seen someone die
Never seen someone die
much less
the love of my life
I go up to bed
in our bedroom
your things everywhere
books
lotions
your phone charger
I lie there
half conscious
There was a detonation
a massive detonation
Everything blew up

Shadow of death
I'm in the rubble
In the rubble
numb
Don't know
if my limbs
are still intact
There was a detonation
a massive detonation
Everything blew up
I'm in the rubble
don't want to get up
see no reason to
I don't know
what time it is
Time has stopped
Start typing on my phone
friends
family
She's gone
She's gone
Repeatedly
over and over
She is gone
Time has stopped
Social media
going nuts
Texts back to me
E-mails
"I didn't even know
she was sick"
a lot of them say
I can't even reply
My phone rings
It's your big boss
He just heard

"I'm sorry
I'm so sorry
If there is anything
I can do"
He starts
to weep
Well not to put
you on the spot
but would you speak
at the funeral?
"Of course I would!
Of course!"
Lying in bed
for hours
I don't know
what just happened
I don't know
A massive detonation
In the rubble
When I finally
go downstairs
my brother is there
I see the bed
the empty hospital bed
Let's get that thing
out of here
I can't look at it
I can't look at it
My phone rings
Hospice
"We can send
a home health aide
over to you tomorrow"
It's too late
she's gone
"We're sorry for your loss"

Thank you
I can't wrap my mind
around that
Checking on expired people
in the middle of the night
driving around
double parking
hazard lights flashing
Shadow of death
The doorbell rings
It's the packet of drugs
that I need to refrigerate
And I laugh

Winter Lake

I awake to the sound
Of angels singing

The night is quiet
Except for the wind

The angels' voices carry
Over miles, across generations

They sing to heal my pain

—from "Angel's Song," a poem in
the book *Diagnosis* by Lenora Lapidus

Pretend

Today
I have to pretend
you are alive
Car registration
in the windshield
fades in the sun
I get a ticket
No registration
Pretend you are alive
I print out
a form
from the DMV website
to get a new one
The car's still registered
in both of our names
so I riffle through
your pocketbook
open your wallet
find your driver's license
write down
your license number
and wait on line
at the pharmacy
to Xerox
both of our licenses
People buying lottery tickets
Even though
I don't play
I want to win the lottery
Pretend you are alive
Because I don't
want the hassle
Don't want

to fill out more forms
Social security numbers
owner title
to present yet another
death certificate
I'm tired of it
I riffle through
your pocketbook
which is mostly empty now
except for your wallet
keys
business cards
Mostly empty now
like a stripped car
When you were a kid
you used to call
your mother's pocketbook
The Blob
So big and stuffed
that she may as well
have lived in it
Like the bottle
in *I Dream of Jeannie*
I wish
I had three wishes
People are still sending me
photos of you
Today I got some
of you in India
two years ago
An endless flight
I study the photos
look for expressions
on your face
that are unfamiliar to me
Learn something new
the smile

the floppy hat
Learn something new
like the puzzled face
on your driver's license
I take the F train
into Manhattan
to the DMV
near Penn Station
Four months
after your death
two days
before school starts
Izzy will be
a senior in high school
I watch a mom
sit with her groggy daughter
hugging her
beach ball on her lap
I think
of you and Izzy
when she was small
We are on the elevated
blue sky
luminous clouds
over Manhattan
The other day
I was flying to Toronto
to visit an old friend
Window seat
I stared
out the window
Clouds
one could bounce on
I think of you
and these clouds
I wish
I could believe in heaven

Pretend you are alive
All goes pretty smoothly
at the DMV
Three bucks
for a new sticker
Later
when I'm coming home
I see some grandparents
by a playground
with a blonde little girl
Grandmother is holding
a milk bottle
Grandfather pushes the stroller
The girl runs off
to chase a ball
They follow fast
"Melanie, wait for us!
Wait for us!"
They seem overwhelmed
awkward at this
first grandchild?
Then I realize
you will never be
a grandmother
Hits me
Goes over
like a medicine ball
Pretend you are alive
I wish
I had three wishes
A stripped car
You will never be
a grandmother
The other day
I found a lighter
in Izzy's laundry
I chuckle

unsure
of how to handle it myself
Unsure
I just text her
Why is it there?
"Found it by the turtle traps
Black Rock Forest"
I should throw it out she says
she meant to give it
to her favorite instructor
Okay
that seems reasonable
I shrug
I wish
I could believe in heaven
Four months
after your death
Thursday will be
Izzy's first day
senior year of high school
We both know
you would have gotten up
with her
at 6 a.m.
Would have snapped the photo
her and her backpack
and water bottle
her pony tail
before she strolled off
to the subway
We both know
you would have gotten up
with her
But this time
it will be me
at 6 a.m.
It will be me

I will regard her
for both of us
Both of us
Snap the photo
Watch her
disappear down the street
And I can pretend
you are alive

Emerge

I call Izzy down
for dinner
Barbequed chicken
with teriyaki sauce
fresh corn
tomatoes, basil
Mozzarella
But she doesn't respond
So I call her cell
"Sorry, I didn't hear you"
She comes down
plops in her chair
"You didn't say goodnight
to me last night"
I saw your door closed
I didn't know if you were asleep
"Doesn't matter
Always say goodnight
You have to"
Okay I will
She's just back
from seven weeks
Summer high school program
at Harvard
And now has internship
Museum of Natural History
Pinkerton Science Scholar
All of these permission forms
that I have to fill out
We both know
that you would have been
the one to fill them out
You would have been

the one
She came home jazzed
from her first day
at the Museum
but now
she's clearly
in a bad mood
I ask her, are you okay?
"I think we should
clean out Mama's study"
Your study or office
in a room
adjacent from Izzy's
but you never really used it
that much
You liked the idea of it
Three illustrations of Buddha
hanging on the wall in front
of your desk
A shelf of law books
feminist literature
"I want to take over the room
and do my work there
But I can't look at the Buddha pictures
We can keep one
I want to replace the desk
and take all of her clothing
out of the closet
and make the room mine
Can we do that?"
Yes
in the fall
Our bedroom
now my bedroom
is mostly you
A walk-in closet
and I have just a corner

It's all of your clothing
that you would rotate
by the season
Dresses
Frilly shirts
Pants
Tons of shoes
Floppy hats
Jewelry
Big silver bracelets
from Santa Fe
Glass earrings
from the island of Murano
Venice
Golden necklaces
my mother made for you
I feel the need
to clean things out too
And it's getting oppressive
and urgent
We need to be able
to move on
or move forward
As my grief counselor puts it
we need to set sail
without you
We need to set sail
"I'm in a bad mood
I can't get anything done
I have too much on my plate"
Izzy says she has work to do
back upstairs
Half her dinner uneaten
I hear her talking I think
maybe her voice breaking
I go upstairs
knock on the door

"Yes?"
Can I come in?
"Sure"
Is there anything
I can do?
"No"
Do you want to talk?
"No, I just have a lot to do
There's a lot on my plate"
It's three months
since you've been gone
and Izzy just came home
for the rest of the summer
And maybe it is the full plate
or maybe more
"Can we do that?"
I have been alone
in the house
most of the summer
I stare at photographs
of us
when we were younger
You cradling Izzy
on your lap
when she was an infant
Cuban money
from your trip to Cuba
three summers ago
You had a blast
A bottle of one
of your precious lotions
And I know
we have to transform the house
Transform
Make it ours
Take it back
Keep a few of your things

but move forward
Take it back
Do you want to talk?
"No"
Is there anything I can do?
"No"
Can we do that?
When I'm on the streets
of New York
with my camera
I pass so many people
look for faces
and juxtapositions
that strike me
So many people
Decrepit ones
with cigarettes
dangling out of their mouths
People engaged
with their phones
Talking
Taking tourist shots
People on crutches
in wheelchairs
lugging suitcases
out of Penn Station
Why can't you be
one of these people?
Still moving
Still circulating
Vital
Striding with purpose
Silly as it is
I look for you
in the crowd
Why can't you be
one of these people?

I hope you will emerge
not like a winged siren
with an enchanting song
a winged ghost
but just you
smiling
wearing loose-fitting clothing
sunglasses
your floppy hat
Smiling
as you stroll
with the others
Emerge
When you were first diagnosed
I used to think
Please, not Izzy
Please, not her
Let me absorb the pain
take the bullet
Izzy is now seventeen
and I know she feels the pain
And I'm helpless
impotent
I wish somehow
I could absorb the punishment
All of the punishment
For Izzy
Absorb it
Take the bullet
Hold her hand
It's okay
It's okay
You don't have to ever feel this
You don't have to ever feel this
Not ever
I look for you
in the crowd

Why can't you be
one of these people?
I look for you
to emerge
Enchanted

Off

Your office
finally shut off your phone
Shut it off
I could probably
access your SIM card
but then
what is the point?
What is the point?
I have everything
I need
I think
Contacts
Passwords
I wanted to save
your voicemail greeting
but I didn't
Didn't
And your voice
was the greeting
on my phone
I had forgotten
until a friend said
"It's creepy
having your dead wife
greet us on voicemail
It's creepy
You should change it"
So I ask
Izzy for help
She is better with technology
than I am
It's creepy
I was afraid

to save it myself
We took three deep breaths
and recorded the cheerful greeting
But I can't
listen to it now
Can't
What is the point?
I saved all of your photos
in the cloud
But I can't
look at them
I can't look
at the photos
I have of you
on my phone
Can't
The last one
I took of you
before you died
you're smiling
with my mother
sister
and Izzy
on my mother's ninetieth
You looked radiant
Big black and gray necklace
Nine days later
no one believed me
that you were fading
No one believed me
"She looked great
just a few days ago"
And my phone
keeps tinging
with alerts
about tropical storms
in other parts

of the country
Like I need
to do something
to act
Even though
on the other side
of the country
off the coast
so far away
It's creepy
What is the point?
I just got an alert
on my phone
Intermittent rain
for the next hour
Rain will be light
Four months
after you're gone
it feels like the first fall day
By the end of the month
a group of us
will go through your belongings
It will be sad
maybe liberating
Feels like the first fall day
I go into our coat closet
to look for
a light jacket
I'm going
to the movies
with a new friend
a theater
I've not been to
since you died
Your office
finally shut off your phone
I've not been to

since you died
I go into our coat closet
to look
for a light jacket
And I forget
it is full of your things
I'm blindsided
Your big black
fluffy winter coat
Your pink rain jacket
that you would wear
for a storm
I imagine you wearing it
with your wide black-rimmed glasses
The coat that Izzy
wants to keep
I can see her
wearing it
Keep it Izzy
Keep it
I can't look
at the photos
I have of you
A hurricane
once came to the Berkshires
our home away from home
right before Labor Day
Everything was closed
Concerts cancelled
Everything shut off
I was standing
on the deck of the house
reassuring you
This isn't so bad
It's not so bad
And then it becomes
eerie quiet

Eerie quiet
It's creepy
I read on my phone
that this is the eye
of the storm
right over us
The eye
This isn't so bad
Everything shut off
And then the wind picks up
Trees thrashing
Pelting rain
Can't even see the lake anymore
Everything under siege
I'm afraid
The trees
are going to snap
You tell me
to come in
Come in
What are you doing out there?
I'm trying to withstand
Withstand
And I think
cancer is like that
It's not so bad
The eerie quiet
and then the real storm
the siege
Everything
is going to snap
including us
I can't look
at the photos
I have of you
I can't
listen to it now

What is the point?
Your office
finally shut off your phone
Shut if off
Mine gets tinging
with alerts
with storms
Everything
is going to snap
Already has
Steve Jobs
once said
that he put
no on/off switch
on his phones
because
he did not like the finality
of that
Did not like the finality
And after he was diagnosed
and dying
wanted to believe
there was an afterlife
So good
that there is no on/off switch
Your office
finally shut off your phone
What is the point?

Miracle

"This is a Hail Mary Pass"
He says it twice
to the two of us
in his office
This is a Hail Mary Pass
Say it to me
not to you
Don't take away your fight
You don't like football
I'm hoping
you don't even know
what a Hail Mary is
that the treatment
for your disease
is a Hail Mary pass
I have never heard a doctor
say this to us before
Never
Your first oncologist
would have never
said this to you
At least
I don't think so
We loved his
bedside manner
how positive he was
literally held your hand
He left
because he was underappreciated
burned out
That was four years ago
This guy
is a different animal

all business
no sugar coating
blunt
wry humor
gray hair
This is ten months
before you are gone
Ten months
Say it to me
not to you
Don't take away your fight
But this all starts
before that
thirteen months
before you are gone
We're to go
to Paris
on Spring Break
the three of us
You keep losing
your breath
winded
I feel weak
I go with you
to see the doctor
I've never met
this new one before
Perlmutter Cancer Center
on 34th Street
I remember
I saw a photographer friend
standing outside
with his camera
Hey, want to come in?
I asked
like the Center was my house
He shook his head

backed away
like I had invited him
to his own execution
Cancer
scares people
You have been
seeing the new doctor
for four years now
Four years
I only come
when there's trouble
When there's trouble
And I sense
we are entering
what I call
a rough patch
This is a Hail Mary Pass
He says it twice
to the two of us
Say it to me
not to you
You don't like football
I'm hoping
you don't even know
what a Hail Mary is
You need
a blood transfusion
Blood levels
are too low
including platelets
tiny blood cells
that help the body
form clots
to stop bleeding
If a blood vessel
gets damaged
sends out signals

to the platelets
They rush to the site
of the damage
form a plug
a clot
You need
a blood transfusion
I hate blood transfusions!
You are over
your fear of them
It's just boring
to sit there
four hours
Part of it
is sitting
in the Infusion Center
and waiting
a long time
for the pharmacy
to deliver
two bags
of blood
320 ml
A second nurse
has to be a witness
to the blood type
and make sure
it's the right one
Patient's date of birth
Two bags
You don't have
to stay here
Go to work
No, I want to stay
It's boring
I want to stay
Two months of this

three transfusions
including one
just for platelets
40 ml
because the levels
are so low
But we do
get to Paris
Selfies
in front of Notre Dame
A Delacroix retrospective
at the Louvre
Walks along the Seine
Shakespeare and Company
The last trip abroad
we will ever take together
The last trip abroad
About six weeks later
blood levels are low again
especially platelets
"I have my suspicions"
Wants a biopsy
from your spine
A biopsy
He looks both concerned
and annoyed
turns to me
frowns
smiles
"Bet you don't want to be here"
I smile back
No place I'd rather be
You need more platelets
Dangerously low
Could bleed to death
No electric toothbrushes
No flossing

No sharp knives
No more subway rides
No walking barefoot
like on a beach
Can I take out my kayak?
No
"Let your husband
chop the vegetables"
Surgeon who is
taking the biopsy
finds it difficult
cutting
into bone
Difficult
Jokes
"You've got some tough bones, ma'am"
Now we're in
your doctor's office
He keeps giving me a look
like I don't seem prepared
for the worst
Don't seem prepared
Keeps giving me a look
shakes his head
You tell him
about the tough bones joke
I only come
when there's trouble
When there's trouble
"That's because
your bone marrow
is full of tumors
It's destroying your blood"
I look at you
You don't seem so bad
I've seen you worse
He's typing furiously

on his computer
I can sense his frustration
almost rage
He will try
a new chemo
half doses at first
pretty much
targets the bone marrow
"But it could kill you"
Your platelets
can drop even lower
cause a heart attack
brain bleeds
It's destroying your blood
This is a Hail Mary Pass
He says it twice
Okay
You made your point
You made your point
"All right, I'll stop saying that"
Don't take away your fight
You don't like football
I'm hoping
you don't even know
what a Hail Mary is
that the treatment
for your disease
is a Hail Mary pass
I have never heard a doctor
say this to us before
Never
Keeps giving me a look
like I don't seem prepared
for the worst
Don't seem prepared
He regards you
bites his lip

"I've never met Izzy
but I feel like I know her
I know you are
protective of her
but I want you to tell her"
Tell her what?
"That you are in a precarious situation
that your life is in grave danger
It could all go very south
Tell a supervisor at work
the same thing"
We're both stunned
"And do yourself a favor
Don't go to work
But I know you
you'll go anyway, right?"
Yup
"What are you doing the week of July 4th?"
We're going to the Berkshires
"No, you're not
I need to monitor you
Sorry"
Sees our frowns
low morale
like we just blew a game
our defeat
"On second thought
maybe it will be good
for you to be in the place
that you love
I changed my mind"
But under certain conditions
every three days
must go to Berkshire Medical Center
for blood tests
that will be sent to NYU
Every three days

"Debbie will write scrips"
Prescriptions
Debbie the nurse practitioner
We leave his office
stand in reception
and try to regroup
to comprehend
You look up at me
into my eyes
Truth
Do you think
I'm going to die?
Do you?
Because I don't
I don't either
even though I'm lying
Fact is
I don't know
Don't know
I'm not a doctor
But this guy seems negative
I hate it
Come to believe
in our own mythology
So many rallies
so many
Thirteen years later
you're still here
He's taking that from us
taking it
I feel angry
scared
You are my best friend
and I can't tell you
I'm scared
What do I do
if this is the end?

What do I do?
Come to believe
in our own mythology
I just want to take out
my kayak this summer
I lie to you
What am I going to say?
Izzy has lots of plans
this summer
including
going to Tanzania
Does everything just stop?
Our instinct
is absolutely not
Let's not say anything
to Izzy yet
We need to think about this
I agree
But we should tell her something
Tell her something
It's destroying your blood
This is a Hail Mary Pass
He says it twice
to the two of us
in his office
This is a Hail Mary Pass
Say it to me
Not to you
Don't take away your fight
I've never heard a doctor
say this to us before
Never
Before we go away
for July 4th week
we sit Izzy down
in her bedroom
The cancer has spread

a bit
I'm doing a treatment
that might be tricky
The doctor
wanted us to tell you
but I know
I'll be alright
Izzy shrugs
"Is that it?
You don't look
so sick to me
You were sicker
when I was younger"
But you should
just know
okay?
Just know
It's destroying your blood
This is a Hail Mary Pass
July 4th
you rest a lot
in the bedroom
The house is full of people
I'm concerned
They don't really know
how serious this is
How serious
You need quiet
I'm concerned
it's too much for you
You can't do a lot
You're weak
I hope the chemo
is working
Is working
We go to the Berkshire Medical Center
in Pittsfield

for blood tests
every three days
They're nice enough there
much less crowded
than NYU
2 a.m. one night
you wake me
My ear really hurts
An earache
It's unbearable
I drive you
to the Emergency Room
We're there all night
mostly waiting
even though it's pretty empty
A nurse tells us
how she is nocturnal
Friends call her
ghost
I just want to take out
my kayak
Too much waiting
I note to myself
Try to avoid Emergency Rooms
Avoid them
They don't know
what's wrong
They are aware of your cancer
give you something
for the pain
When we see
your doctor in New York
he thinks
it was unrelated
to the cancer
or the chemo
"It's a fluke"

Blood labs are back
platelets slightly up
Is it working?
Is it working?
"I don't know
Maybe, okay?
I'll give you a maybe"
The next week
we come back
Platelets
up again
Is this for real?
Debbie the nurse practitioner
visibly excited
The doctor smiles
"I think it may be, okay?
It may be"
Izzy goes off
with her friend
A program in Tanzania
two weeks in August
Big send-off
at JFK
She'll be far away
This isn't like
sending her to summer camp
She texts
when she arrives
by way of Qatar
Relieved she's with a friend
we text back
But we don't know
that our texts
aren't getting to her
We're sitting
at the lake
when your phone rings

from a strange number
She calls us
from Tanzania
sounds like
she's next door
"Is everything okay?
Why aren't you answering my texts?"
We are
but I guess
they're not going through
Everything is fine
"I thought something
bad happened"
No
It's all good
All good
She tells us
how she feels like
she entered
a National Geographic magazine
"I love it here
I'm learning Swahili"
And the platelets
keep going up
We're so relieved
practically high-fiving
like we won the big one
Won the big one
Somebody caught
the Hail Mary Pass
By the end
of the summer
you are able
to go in your kayak
Eight months
before you're gone
It is to be

your last kayak ride
Last one
Labor Day weekend
Don't you want
To come with me?
I don't
Because then I have
to lug two kayaks
from our garage
and put them back
the same weekend
We get permission
from our neighbors
across the street
to put the kayak in
from their yard
I carry it down
steady it for you
as you step in
Be careful
And you sit
Your big sunglasses
Floppy hat
I hand you the paddle
Take pictures, I say
I will
And enjoy
Oh, I will
The lake is pulsing
throwing light everywhere
rich blue
in front of soothing hills
Rhythm abounds
Oh, I didn't tell you
The doctor called me today
Platelets are at 80,000
We started at 19,000

Normal is between
150,000 and 450,000
He called me his miracle patient
You wink
and start to paddle away
I'll wait for you
You know where
my chair
the common dock
I watch you paddle
past a little family of ducks
You paddle with the current
I can see you
regarding everything
The sky
The clouds
The expanse of water
A miracle

End Notes

Lenora Michelle Lapidus
(17 May 1963 – 5 May 2019)

May—usually my favorite month
The smell of spring in the air
Warm sun shining brightly
Long days spanning into night

—from "The Month of May," a poem in
    the book *Diagnosis* by Lenora Lapidus

From the ACLU Women's Rights Project

Lenora M. Lapidus, who for nearly two decades led the women's rights program at the American Civil Liberties Union once helmed by Ruth Bader Ginsburg, died on May 5, 2019, of cancer. She was 55.

Ms. Lapidus's career as an advocate for women and girls spanned three decades, most of it spent with the ACLU. It began in the summer of 1988, when Ms. Lapidus was a law student intern with the organization's Women's Rights Project (WRP). Co-founded in 1971 by now-Supreme Court Justice Ginsburg, WRP had won numerous landmark Supreme Court rulings throughout the 1970s that established women's rights under the U.S. Constitution. Twelve years after her internship, in 2001, Ms. Lapidus returned to WRP as its Director, having already served as the top lawyer with the ACLU's New Jersey affiliate.

By the time Ms. Lapidus took over, WRP had ceased active litigation, but she revived it and grew it to nearly a dozen staff members, pursuing an ambitious litigation and policy agenda targeting a broad range of economic and social justice issues that yielded victories in the Supreme Court, the Inter-American Commission on Human Rights, and countless federal, state, and local courts and legislatures. At the ACLU, we are fond of saying that Lenora Lapidus renovated the house that Justice Ruth Bader Ginsburg built.

[...]

Ms. Lapidus's expansive vision for women's rights was legendary. Under [her] leadership, WRP entered legal territory not traditionally occupied by gender justice groups. In 2013, it secured a unanimous ruling in Association for Molecular Pathology v. Myriad Genetics, a landmark challenge to the patenting of human genes linked to hereditary risk for breast and ovarian cancers.... The Court's ruling assured that genetic testing that could benefit millions would not be impeded by corporate ownership of selected genes.

[…]

Ms. Lapidus long cited as inspiration Justice Ginsburg's commitment, as a WRP litigator, to dismantling sex stereotypes not only on the job or in the classroom, but also at home. On a recent episode of the ACLU podcast, "At Liberty," Ms. Lapidus reminisced about meeting with Justice Ginsburg before assuming the mantle of WRP Director, and asking her what she considered the greatest modern challenges for gender justice. Justice Ginsburg observed to her that while women had broken many barriers in the workplace, men had not yet broken those barriers in the home. In keeping with that mission, Ms. Lapidus's team recently sued J.P. Morgan Chase to challenge as sex discrimination its presumption that only birth mothers could serve as primary caregivers for purposes of enjoying full parental leave benefits, a disparity rooted in time-worn notions of who is, and is not, the primary caregiver in families.

[…]

Ms. Lapidus was defined by her fierce tenacity, her generosity of spirit, her boundless optimism, her joy in life, and her commitment to her family. She was someone who demanded freedom and justice, and she was a force to be reckoned with. She cared deeply about mentorship, and about fostering the next generation of feminist attorneys and activists. She provided invaluable support, training, and mentorship to a host of young women lawyers and to the staff at ACLU. We will miss her terribly. But having learned from her, and continuing to be inspired by her indomitable spirit, we are even more committed to building on her legacy.

—Full article "From the ACLU Women's Rights Project" may be accessed in Volume 43 of *The Harbinger* (an online-only publication of *The N.Y.U. Review of Law & Social Change*) at:
https://socialchangenyu.com/harbinger/tribute-to-lenora-lapidus/

Excerpts reprinted by permission of American Civil Liberties Union.

About the Author

Matt Bialer is the author of more than a dozen books of poetry including *Radius* (Les Editions du Zaporogue); *Already Here, Ark,* and *Black Powder* (three from Black Coffee Press); *Bridge, The Valley of the Eight,* and *Third Eye of the Inner Light* (three from Leaky Boot Press); *Tell Them What I Saw* (PS Publishing, UK); *Formation* (Weirdo Magnet); *He Walks On All Fours* (Dynatox Ministries); and *Ascent* and *Wonder Weavers* (two from Bizarro Pulp Press). His poems have appeared in numerous print and online journals including *Bareknuckle Poet, Cultural Weekly, Forklift Ohio, Gobbet, Green Mountains Review, H_NGM_N, La Zaporogue,* and *MacQueen's Quinterly.*

In addition, Matt's an acclaimed street photographer (primarily black-and-white) and an accomplished painter of watercolor landscapes who has exhibited his works widely. Some of his photographs are held in the permanent collections of The Brooklyn Museum, The Museum of the City of New York, and the The New York Public Library, and his watercolors reside in many private collections. His photographic monographs, *A Moment's Notice* (with foreword by D. Foy) and *More Than You Know,* were published by Les Editions du Zaporogue in 2016 and 2011, respectively. The same publisher issued a book of his paintings in 2012, *Shadowbrook.*

Author's website: www.mattbialer.com

Acknowledgments

Thank you to Clare MacQueen of KYSO Flash Press for believing in this project and for bringing your vision and editing to this book.

Thank you to all of my firefighter and builder friends and family who have been in my corner, had my back. Firefighters are the friends who drop what they are doing and jump into the fray by your side. And then there is the reconstruction crew—the builders—those whose calm, steady care will help you regain your footing in the world. Big thank you.

Thank you to my parents Irving and Thelma Bialer, my brother David Bialer, sister Roni Fontaine, and Mary McNear, Michael Gill, Rose Bialer, and Harry Bialer. I love you all.

And for help with these poems in terms of feedback, encouragement, and cheerleading, huge thanks to:

Seb Doubinsky, Matthew Rohrer, Sharon Guskin, Jennifer Zitron Soumi, Alexis Rhone Fancher, Loretta Oleck, Matthew Lippman, Susan Skolnick, Cynthia Atkins, Nancy Jean Burns, Andrea Slane, Kirsten Towers, Maddy Jacobs, Carla Savetsky, Samantha Anderson, Jenny Kinder, Karen Dublin, Jane von Mehren, Scott Miller, Suzanne Wise, Elizabeth Powell, Elizabeth Cohen, Prageeta Sharma, Hollis Kurman, and Lynn Hightower.

Special thanks to Alicia Brooks and her unwavering support and belief. She also plucked the title of this collection from my poem "Emerge" [see page 114].

And, finally, thank you to Anthony Romero, Louise Melling, Galen Sherwin, and Sandra Park of the ACLU. I know Lenora's fighting and generous spirit lives on in you.

—Matt Bialer
November 2019

Credits

"Island" is reprinted from *MacQueen's Quinterly* online (Issue 1, January 2020).

"More Things I Would Tell You" is forthcoming in early 2020 in *Green Mountains Review*.

Blurbs at the front of this book and on the back cover are copyrighted by their respective authors and appear herein with their permissions.

Pages 12, 14, 107, 144, and 150: Quotations from poems by Lenora Lapidus appear with permissions from Matt Bialer and Leaky Boot Press, publisher of Lenora's book of poems, *Diagnosis* (2013).

Photographs and Paintings appear herein with permission from the author and artist, Matt Bialer.

Page 57: Photograph of water lilies and bow of red kayak by Lenora Lapidus, and now copyrighted © by Matt Bialer. All rights reserved.

Page 63: Untitled watercolor painting by Matt Bialer. Copyrighted © by the artist. All rights reserved.

Page 107: *Winter Lake*, watercolor painting copyrighted © 2019 by the artist, Matt Bialer. All rights reserved.

Page 143: Photograph of Lenora Michelle Lapidus is reproduced here with kind permission from the ACLU, American Civil Liberties Union. (Licensing agreement dated 14 November 2019.) All rights reserved.

Page 151: Photograph of Lenora Lapidus and Isabel Bialer Lapidus is copyrighted © 2005 by Matt Bialer, all rights reserved, and reproduced herein with his permission.

Thoughts
      of Isabel
            of Matt

of the everyday world
Then no thoughts at all
      just floating

Somewhere deep
      somewhere calm

—from "Reiki," a poem in the book
   Diagnosis by Lenora Lapidus

Cover Photograph

Lenora and Izzy, 2005

Photograph copyrighted © by Matt Bialer. All rights reserved.
An abstract version appears on the front cover of this book.

About the Editor and Publisher

Clare MacQueen served as webmaster and copy editor for 18 issues of *Serving House Journal* from its launch online in 2010 to its retirement in 2018. She co-edited *Steve Kowit: This Unspeakably Marvelous Life* (Serving House Books, 2015). She's founding editor and publisher of the new online literary journal *MacQueen's Quinterly* (aka MacQ); and co-editor, webmaster, and publisher of *KYSO Flash*, the online literary journal and micro-press that she founded in 2014 in memory of her daughter, Kelley M. Smith. Both journals, *KYSO Flash* and MacQ, celebrate a smorgasbord of short-form writings and visual arts.

Via KYSO Flash Press, Clare has designed and produced 20 print books, including anthologies and short-form collections for writers and artists whose works have been published in her journals online. Her own essays, reviews, stories, and poems have appeared in, among others, *New Flash Fiction Review, Ribbons, Serving House Journal, Skylark,* and the anthologies *Best New Writing 2007* (Hopewell Publications) and *Winter Tales II: Women on the Art of Aging* (Serving House Books, 2012).

www.kysoflash.com

an online literary journal &
a micro-press of printed books

Knock-Your-Socks-Off Art and Literature